AF254820

I Adore You

Finding Hope and a Home in a New Land

Written by
Fardous Hosseiny
Jaihoon Nawzadi

Illustrated by
Emmeline Keeling

To my son, Daniyal Fardous Hosseiny - F.H.

I started my days with some bread and some tea

The breakfast my mother always made for me
We sat at the table and dad would join too
For many years this was the life that we knew.

I put on my backpack, my shoes and my glasses

My mom held my hand and walked me to my classes
She held me on one side, and in my other hand
Was my dear teddy bear, my companion and friend.

Teddy and I went to sleep every night

Excited to wake in the bright morning light
But just when we thought we had peace in our lives
Everything changed to all of our surprise.

I woke up one day and I walked to the kitchen
Dad hugged me like always, but this hug felt different
We turned on the news, jaws dropped to the floor
Our country is in danger, they say we are at war.

Suddenly, I couldn't leave home, eat or sleep

All I could hear was the noise in the streets
The sounds I could hear from outside made me wonder
The skies are still blue but I thought I heard thunder.

My dad sat next to me and said "we are leaving"
I packed all my things and we left before evening
I sat on the plane, and although I didn't feel ready
I still had my mom and my dad and my teddy.

When we got off the plane, I looked into the streets
The cars on the road were so shiny and sleek
This place was so different than Kabul, my home
But I felt so excited to call this place my own.

I entered my school for the very first time

The walls were all painted with different designs
I dreamt about pencils and pens to call mine
To touch them to notebooks and draw perfect lines.

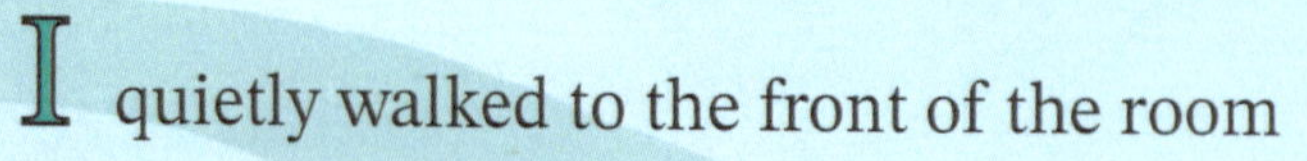

I quietly walked to the front of the room

I hoped my new classmates would be my friends soon
I heard them all giggling, but what was it for?
I told them my name – they laughed even more.

I felt so embarrassed, I ran to the door

I've never been laughed at for my name before.
Teddy, why did they laugh over something so little?
My name is a name, not a joke or a riddle.

Oh Sana! I'll tell you something that they may not know
Your name is so special; it means something that "glows"
Your name is so great, it should not be concealed
Its power and beauty should all be revealed!

Today my new friend saw the scarf on my head

She told me she liked it – "it is pretty and red"
She asked why I don't let my hair hang out instead
I said, "It is my hijab" ... what else could I have said?

Sana, if they only knew
Your mother wears a scarf and your grandmother too.
They loved wearing theirs so they gave one to you
Your scarf is for modesty —that is its goal
It lets people focus on your beautiful soul.

I adore the hijab that you wear every day
Some people don't wear one and that too is okay
One thing that you will learn is that people are different
We have different colours, shapes and conditions.

We have different interests and make different decisions
There are different religions and different traditions
Some people wear yamikahs, some people bracelets
Some people wear hats, but your scarf is my favourite.

Today, my dad and I came to the mall

As I looked around, I felt oh so small
Then something I noticed when I looked up from my view
The people in here – they look different than I do.

I look at them, then myself, and start to compare

My features are darker, my skin and my hair
I do not want to look different, it doesn't seem fair
Why are mine all so different than theirs?

Sana, the way that we look from the outside
Is not something that we control
What matters is who is inside you.
That person is known as your soul.

Everyone looks a bit different, it's true
But we shouldn't fear something just because it is new
When you meet someone, just look at their soul
And see them as part of a beautiful whole.

After awhile I started to finally feel settled

I was making more friends and my English was better
I was speaking to people more easily too
In my heart I just knew, this place is my place, my home through and through.

One day I had to go to the doctor and leave class a bit early
My mom came to get me, her dress so colourful and pearly
She said "Salam"
I said "Hi, Mom"

When we got in the car, my mom seemed upset and I could not understand it
She said to me "I said Salam, but you did not reply in our language."

Sana, your parents spent days, even weeks,
Sharing their words, teaching you to speak.
The language they love is a gift from their heart,
But they see your English is sharp from the start.

Your progress is shining, a beautiful sight,
Keep learning your English; it's your guiding light.
But your mother speaks with a voice full of care,
Show her your love—speak the language you share.

These days, my dad has been working much more

So, I went to go visit his job at the store
When I walked through the door, it was to my surprise
I saw one of my friends, who had wide-open eyes.

Sana, when she saw your dad there mopping the floor
She just didn't know he was a doctor before
He had tools and a white coat that he always wore
He took care of the patients that walked through his door.

But it was you and your family he left all that for,
Your dad feels such joy when he walks through the door.
He loves to work for, to clothe and to feed you
You are his passion, you are so lucky - believe it, it's true!

W hen I first moved here and boarded that flight

I had such dreams in my heart, I was filled with delight
But then I met people who seemed so much different from me.
They thought I was strange, and I thought so too you see.

I remember the struggle, the anger and fright

But talking to teddy every single night
The more that I realized what truly is right
The more that I realized the truth and the light.

My culture, my clothing, my skin and my name

Make me unique and different, but still me all the same
These are all things they may not understand
But all of these things are what make me who I am.

I thought all the things that were different about me

Were things I should change so that I could be happy
But in fact I was wrong, because they make me strong
And despite all these differences I can still belong.

I woke up one day and my life was in danger

I moved to a new place and I felt like a stranger
But my teddy told me to look in the mirror
And say "Sana is special and nothing will change her".

So now, I wake up and I love who I am

There's nobody out there that I am lesser than
I cherish all others and extend my hand
For we are all friends in this wonderful land.

I adore you!